Wackysaurus

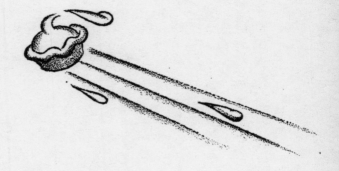

Wackysaurus

DINOSAUR JOKES

by LOUIS PHILLIPS
illustrated by RON BARRETT

A TRUMPET CLUB SPECIAL EDITION

for

Elizabeth Berger

Oona Curley

Tamara Martin

—L.P.

Published by The Trumpet Club
1540 Broadway, New York, New York 10036

Text copyright © Louis Phillips, 1991
Illustrations copyright © Ron Barrett, 1991

ISBN 0-440-83291-8

This edition published by arrangement with Viking Penguin,
a division of Penguin Books USA Inc.

Set in Palatino
Printed in the United States of America
February 1994
1 3 5 7 9 10 8 6 4 2
OPM

CONTENTS

CHAPTER ONE

Here Come the Dinosaurs!

NANCY: I'm going to write my school report on the topic of the life of the parasaurolophus.

LAUREN: Spell it.

NANCY: I've changed my mind. I think I'll write about the life of my cat.

BETTY: Remember, Beau, never pull a dinosaur's tail.

BEAU: Why not?

BETTY: Because to the dinosaur it's just a tail, but to you it could be the end.

PAUL: Is it true that if I carry a long pole, dinosaurs will not attack me?

JEAN: It depends on how fast you carry the pole.

What is yellow on the outside and dark green on the inside?

A tyrannosaurus rex in a taxi.

What would you have if a herd of dinosaurs ran over
Batman and Robin?

　　You'd get Flatman and Ribbon.

How can you tell the difference between a dinosaur and an
elephant?

　　A dinosaur always forgets.

What has a horn, weighs seven or eight tons, is about
30 feet long, and goes up and down, up and down,
up and down, up and down?

　　A triceratops yo-yo.

Let's try that one again. What has a horn, weighs seven or
eight tons, is about 30 feet long, and goes up and down,
up and down, up and down?

　　A triceratops on a pogo stick.

One more time: What has a horn, weighs seven or eight
tons, is about 30 feet long, and goes up and down, up and
down, up and down?

　　A triceratops elevator operator.

ALEXANDRA: What is green and sour
　　and weighs over 5 tons?
LINDA: Picklesaurus.

FAMOUS DINOSAUR QUOTATIONS

A rolling dinosaur gathers no moss.

People who live in glass houses with pet dinosaurs rarely get much sleep.

Red dinosaur at morning, sailor take warning.

A dinosaur in the hand may not be worth two in the bush, but it does mean that you have a very, very large hand.

Anger a dinosaur in haste, repent in leisure—if you are in any state to repent at all!

You can lead a dinosaur to water, but you can't make it drink. On the other hand, if you can lead a dinosaur to water, you can probably get it to do whatever you want.

Why did the dinosaur cross the road?
　　It was the chicken's day off!

Why did the dinosaur cross the road?
　　Because it was tied to the chicken's right leg!

ANNIE: Why did the dinosaur cross the road?
MISSY: I give up. Why did the dinosaur cross the
　　road?
ANNIE: To get his copy of *The Hong Kong Weekly
　　Newspaper*.
MISSY: I don't get it.
ANNIE: I don't get it either. I read *The New York
　　Times*.

KAY: Why did the dinosaur cross the road?
BOB: I give up. Why did the dinosaur cross the road?
KAY: To collect his social security check.
BOB: To collect his social security check? I don't
　　get it.
KAY: Neither did he.

JANE: What kind of dinosaur had the shortest legs?
JUDY: The smallest one.

DINOSAUR #1: Sometimes I think I'm invisible.
DINOSAUR #2: Who said that?

IAN: If a dinosaur falls off a cliff, what would he fall
　　against?
MATTHEW: Against his will.

KATEY: If you have three dinosaurs in your bedroom, two dinosaurs in your living room, and three dinosaurs in your kitchen, what do you have?

JOHN: What?

KATEY: A very, very messy house.

JOHN: If you have three dinosaurs in your bedroom, two dinosaurs in your living room, and three dinosaurs in your kitchen, what do you have?

KATEY: What?

JOHN: A very, very large house.

DINO-MATH

$$
\begin{array}{r}
\text{Nickeltrodon} \\
+ \text{Nickeltrodon} \\
\hline
\text{Dimetrodon}
\end{array}
$$

What do you find between the toes of a haplocanthosaurus?
   Slow-running hunters.

Why did the dinosaur paint itself green, brown, yellow, and orange?

So it could hide in a package of M&M's and not be seen.

How can you fit four dinosaurs inside your car?

Put two in the front seat and two in the backseat.

A long, long, time ago—okay, it only happened yesterday—all the major dinosaurs who loved football decided to form their own team and play any other team of animals that dared to take them on. The games went on for days, for weeks, for months. At last the Pleistocene Super Bowl came down to two great teams: the Minnesota Dinosaurs vs. the Tar Pit Ants.

The ants won the coin toss and elected to receive. The first quarter was nip and tuck. The second quarter was ferocious and close to violent. By the end of the first half, the score was 10–10. The fans were delirious with anticipation. At least the ant fans were delirious with anticipation.

In the third quarter and through most of the fourth quarter, both teams were held scoreless. Try as they might, the great dinosaur football team could not break through the stubborn defense of the ants. The ants were tiny but they played smart.

Finally there were only four minutes left to play. The ants had the ball on the one-yard line of the dinosaurs. The insect fans shouted for a touchdown. The cheerleaders went all out.

---

*T*he quarterback for the ants—Joe Namant—tried to sneak over the defensive line, but when it looked as if he were going to score, one of the mighty brontosaurus linemen lifted up his great foot and squashed the ant to the ground.

The referee blew his whistle. He rushed over to the mighty brontosaurus. "You killed the ant! That will be a twenty-yard penalty for roughing the quarterback."

"But I didn't mean to kill him," the brontosaurus said. "I was just trying to trip him!"

A man entered a store that sold exotic foods. Behind the counter there was a sign that read:

One pound of horse brains—$30
One pound of cow brains—$40
One pound of dinosaur brains—$46,000

"Wait a minute," the man said. "How come dinosaur brains are so much more expensive than all the other animals' brains?"

"Do you know how many dinosaurs it takes to make a pound of brains?"

A woman entered a restaurant featuring an unusual menu. After being seated by the headwaiter, the woman took up the menu and read:

> *Elephant Brain—$1.00*
> *Fox Brain—$2.00*
> *Hippopotamus Brain—$3.00*
> *Dinosaur Brain—$897.50*

Not only was the woman astonished to find dinosaur brain featured on the menu, she was also quite taken aback by the price. She called the headwaiter over to ask, "Could you please tell me why dinosaur brain is so expensive?"

"Because it was never used, madam. It's as good as new."

Why don't dinosaurs go bowling on Saturday night?
    Because no one has size 3000x bowling shoes.

TEACHER: How do you spell *dinosaur?*
IAN: D-I-N-O-S-A-U . . .
TEACHER: Go on, what's at the end of it?
IAN: Its tail!

Why do dinosaurs have wrinkled knees?
    Because they can't find an iron to get them pressed.

Knock, knock.
Who's there?
Dinosaur.
Dinosaur who?
    Dinosaur (Dinah's sore) that you didn't invite her to the party.

How can you tell that there's a dinosaur in the bathtub?
    You can't get the shower curtain closed.

Why couldn't the dinosaur in the swamp attend a birthday party for his friend?
    He was bogged down in his work.

What was the fossil collector doing during her final week at school?
    Boning up for her final exams.

Why do most dinosaurs have such pointed tails?
From standing too close to the pencil sharpener.

Why is the Liberty Bell like a bad dinosaur egg?
Because they're both cracked.

Why were dinosaurs always exhausted in April?
Because they had just finished a long march of 31 days.

Why are dinosaurs huge and purple?
Because if they were small and white, they would be aspirin tablets.

YOUR SAUROSCOPE!

AQUASERIOUS (Jan. 20–Feb. 18) If your birth falls under the sign of AQUASERIOUS, then you never laugh at a bowl of water. You also know that the *trachodon* had more than 2,000 teeth, but what good such knowledge does you is difficult to say.

PISCESCELARIUS (Feb. 19–March 20) You are destined to play tuba or trumpet, like the *protoceratops*, whose name means "first hornface." These horns will bother you at first; then, later, you will play them in a dance band.

STEGO-ARIES (March 21–April 19) Start your day on a positive note: take a *stegosaurus* to breakfast. (If you can afford to do that, then you are really well-off.)

CAMPTO-TAURUS (April 20–May 20) Since your legs are heavy and short, you should beware of going anywhere with an *apatosaurus*. Traveling with an *apatosaurus* could wear you out, especially if you have to carry all the baggage.

CENOZEMINI (May 21–June 21) An unexpected visit from twin *brachiosauruses* could wreck your weekend—not to mention your house! Each *brachiosaurus* measures 90 feet long, so be sure that your guest bed is adequate.

ALLOSACANCERUS (June 22–July 22) You should sweep the *allosaurus* (that "other lizard") out of your life. Although the *allosaurus* has a big head, it is really not witty enough to carry on an extended conversation. Since the beast is nearly 35 feet long, you could, however, talk about that.

LEOSAURUS (July 23–August 22) You should try to keep the lines of communication open between you and any lambeosaurid friends.

BRACHIOVIRGO (August 23–September 22) Trust your intincts. You can get the edge on any competitors by breeding a new *brachiosaurus*. Streamline this heavy dinosaur by going on a weight-loss diet with it.

LIBRASAURUS (September 23–October 23) Be more considerate of the "ancient feather" or *archaeopteryx*. If you are asked to spell *archaeopteryx* in a spelling bee, rethink the rest of your education.

SCORPIODONTIST (October 24–November 21) Your best career choice would be dentistry. You can help that *camptosaurus* you've been friendly with. Since its teeth are set far back in its mouth, you could bring them out into the open where everybody could enjoy them.

SAGITTARISAURUS (November 22–December 21) A ride on the back of a *megalosaurus* will make you the envy of your friends. Watch out for its teeth, or you could make your enemies happy also.

CAPRICORNUSAURUS (December 22–January 19) You will spend next summer swimming with a *trachodon*. Don't make fun of its webbed feet, however, or you will wish you had gone mountain climbing.

Knock, knock.
Who's there?
Hair comb.
Hair comb who?
    Hair comb some more dinosaurs.

CHAPTER TWO

The Big Ones

Brontosaurus Meets
Tyrannosaurus Rex

BETTY: How come the brontosaurus had such a long neck?

BEAU: Because its head was so far from its body.

BRONTOSAURUS #1: Are you Hungary?

BRONTOSAURUS #2: Yes, Siam.

BRONTOSAURUS #1: Okay, I'll Fiji.

BRONTOSAURUS #2: Denmark down what we're going to eat.

BRONTOSAURUS #1: How about a Cuba sugar?

TYRANNOSAURUS REX #1: Come over here, Camera.

TYRANNOSAURUS REX #2: Why do you call me Camera?

TYRANNOSAURUS REX #1: Because you're always snapping at me.

TYRANNOSAURUS REX #1: How many dinosaurs can dance on the head of the pin?

TYRANNOSAURUS REX #2: I don't know. How many?

TYRANNOSAURUS REX #1: Fifty.

TYRANNOSAURUS REX #2: Fifty?

TYRANNOSAURUS REX #1: But it has to be a very large pin.

What did the tyrannosaurus rex do after he drank up all the water in Toronto?

Oh, he started to drink Canada Dry.

How tall is a tyrannosaurus rex?

I don't know, but he's always above two feet.

MOMMA TYRANNOSAURUS REX: Alfred, I'm worried about our son.

POPPA TYRANNOSAURUS REX: Why?

MOMMA TYRANNOSAURUS REX: He thinks he's a chicken.

POPPA TYRANNOSAURUS REX: That's terrible! We had better take him to the doctor right away.

MOMMA TYRANNOSAURUS REX: No, let's wait a few days. We may need the eggs.

What do you call a very rich brontosaurus?
A gold-blooded reptile.

What goes "ha ha ha ha ha ha" plop?
A brontosaurus laughing his head off.

BRONTOSAURUS: What's wrong with me? I go around all day with my tongue hanging out.

DOCTOR: Just a minute. I've got some stamps that need licking.

BRONTOSAURUS, JR.: Momma, Momma! But I don't want to go to Australia.

BRONTOSAURUS MOTHER: Shut up and keep swimming.

Knock, knock.
Who's there?
Brontosaurus.
Brontosaurus who?

Brontosaurus taking cookies from the cookie jar.
(Bronto saw us . . .)

BIG BRONTOSAURUS: I think we've just stepped into quicksand.

LITTLE BRONTOSAURUS: I'm getting that sinking feeling myself.

STEGOSAURUS: How did you get so tall?

BRONTOSAURUS: I rubbed grease on my head.

STEGOSAURUS: I rubbed grease on my head, too, but I didn't get any taller.

BRONTOSAURUS: What kind of grease did you use?

STEGOSAURUS: Crisco.

BRONTOSAURUS: Well, no wonder. You used shortening.

Ruth rode a tyrannosaurus rex
Directly back of me;
We hit a bump at sixty-five
And rode on ruthlessly.

TYRANNOSAURUS REX JR.: Am I late for dinner?

MOTHER TYRANNOSAURUS REX: Yes, everybody's been eaten.

TYRANNOSAURUS REX #1: It's driving me crazy.

TYRANNOSAURUS REX #2: What?

TYRANNOSAURUS REX #1: I can't remember anything more than a few seconds at a time.

TYRANNOSAURUS REX #2: How long has that been going on?

TYRANNOSAURUS REX #1: How long has what been going on?

TYRANNOSAURUS REX: Do you want some beans for supper?
TYRANNOSAURUS REX, JR.: Beans?
TYRANNOSAURUS REX: Human beans?

KAREN: What game does the tyrannosaurus rex like to play with human beings?
NANCY: What?
KAREN: Squash.

What do you call a brontosaurus who stayed out all night in the rain?
Brontosaurust.

TYRANNOSAURUS REX: I go around all day thinking I'm a rubber band.
BRONTOSAURUS: Snap out of it.

*T*here were two famous hunters and they had shot every kind of animal—every kind of animal, that is, except a tyrannosaurus rex. The hunter named Jones turned to his friend and said, "I'll bet you a thousand dollars that I can kill a tyrannosaurus rex and I'm going to do it within the hour."

"You're on!" Jones's friend said.

And so Jones went off into the jungle. About 45 minutes later, a huge tyrannosaurus rex came lumbering out of the jungle. "Do you know a hunter named Jones?" it asked.

Jones's friend, scared to death, dropped his gun and fell to his knees. His teeth chattered. His hand trembled. "Y-Y-Yes . . . Yes. I know a hunter named Jones."

"Well, he owes you a thousand dollars."

BRONTOSAURUS: Do you really like living in that tiny cave?
TYRANNOSAURUS REX: Sure. I have no room to complain.

BRONTOSAURUS: Why are you wearing that sailor's cap?
TYRANNOSAURUS REX: Because I'm a war baby, that's why.
BRONTOSAURUS: Come off it. You're no war baby.
TYRANNOSAURUS REX: Oh, yeah? The minute I was born, my parents took one look at me and started fighting.

BRONTOSAURUS: Why is your head all bandaged?
TYRANNOSAURUS REX: Because when I went inside
the antique store, I asked, "What's new?"

BRONTOSAURUS #1: What have you been doing
all day?
BRONTOSAURUS #2: I just ate 3,309 cakes made with
batter, eggs, and milk. What do you say to that?
BRONTOSAURUS #1: How waffle!

BRONTOSAURUS #1: Yoo-hoo.
BRONTOSAURUS #2: Yes, what is it?
BRONTOSAURUS #1: Your husband was just run over
by a steamroller.
BRONTOSAURUS #2: Just slip him under the door.

MRS. BRONTOSAURUS TO JUNIOR: If you fall off that rock and break your legs, don't come running to me.

What dinosaur wrote Jane Eyre?
Charlotte Bronte-saurus.

What do you get if you cross a brontosaurus with a kangaroo?
Potholes the size of Rhode Island.

BUDDY: Is it difficult to bury a dead brontosaurus?
FRAN: Yes, it's a huge undertaking.

BRONTOSAURUS #1: Are you using your claws to dig huge trenches?
BRONTOSAURUS #2: No.
BRONTOSAURUS #1: Why not?
BRONTOSAURUS #2: Because I'm tired of the hole business.

BRONTOSAURUS #1: That hunter over there shot me in the leg last year.
BRONTOSAURUS #2: Have a scar?
BRONTOSAURUS #1: No, thanks, I don't smoke.

MORTY: I saw a 90-year-old brontosaurus climbing a mountain.

LINDA: It shouldn't do that.

MORTY: Why not?

LINDA: Because a 90-year-old brontosaurus is past its peak.

BRONTOSAURUS: Mommy, come quick! I just saw a tyrannosaurus rex fall off a cliff.

MOTHER BRONTOSAURUS: How terrible! Is the tyrannosaurus hurt?

BRONTOSAURUS: I don't know. He hadn't finished falling when I left.

CHAPTER THREE

What's Up, Diplodocus?

Why did the diplodocus sit on the pumpkin?
    He wanted to play squash.

How do you make a diplodocus sandwich?
    First, you start with two very large
pieces of bread.

Knock, knock.
Who's there?
Diplodocus.
Diplodocus who?
    CRUNCH!

What is 80 feet long and lights up?
    A diplodocus lamp.

What do you do with a blue diplodocus?
    Cheer it up.

Why is the diplodocus such a bad dancer?
    He has two left feet.

MIKE: Should a diplodocus swim on a full stomach?
JOAN: No. It's much better if he swims on water.

DEBORAH: What do you call a person who is brave enough to stick his right hand into the mouth of a diplodocus?
RACHEL: Lefty.

ISAAC: You've heard of hot-dog stands.
How do you make a diplodocus stand?
AUGUSTA: Take away his chair.

PETE: How do you call a diplodocus?
EMILY: Well, first you have to look up its number in a phone directory.
PETE: Come on, be serious. How do you call a diplodocus?
EMILY: I give up. How?
PETE: From a long way off.

JANE: How come a diplodocus isn't yellow?
JOAN: So you don't confuse it with a banana.

JOAN: What did the caveman yell?
JANE: Here come the bananas!
JOAN: Why would he do a silly thing like that?
JANE: Because he was color-blind.

JOAN: Okay, then why did the diplodocus wear a yellow bathrobe to the Halloween party?
JANE: Because he was going to the party disguised as a banana.

JANE: Very well, then what goes *snap, crackle, pop, ouch!?*

JOAN: A Rice Krispie being trampled by a diplodocus.

What is a foolish diplodocus called?
    A dopelodocus.

NANCY: Pardon me, I'm looking for a diplodocus with one eye.

LAUREN: Wouldn't it be better if you looked for it with both eyes?

DIPLODOCUS #1: Your stomach's too fat. You're going to have to diet.

DIPLODOCUS #2: Okay. But what color?

DIPLODOCUS #1: I thought you were going to take the shell off that coconut before you ate it.

DIPLODOCUS #2: It wasn't necessary. I already knew what was inside it.

OONA: Why did the silly diplodocus sit on a marshmallow?

ANNIE: Why?

OONA: To keep from falling into the hot chocolate.

CHAPTER FOUR

Waiter, There's a Dinosaur in My Soup!

Why do waiters like dinosaurs better than flies?

Have you ever heard of a customer complaining, "Waiter! There's a dinosaur in my soup?"

Hold on to your hats, because now you will . . .

CUSTOMER IN A RESTAURANT: Waiter, there's a dinosaur in my soup.

WAITER: Don't worry, sir. I'll take it back to the chef and exchange it for a fly.

CUSTOMER IN A RESTAURANT: Waiter, what's this dinosaur doing in my soup?

WAITER: Looks like it's wading, sir.

CUSTOMER IN A RESTAURANT: Waiter, there's a dead dinosaur in my soup—

WAITER: Of course it's dead. What do you want? It's been extinct for millions of years!

CUSTOMER IN A RESTAURANT: Waiter, there's a fly in my soup.

WAITER: So, what's the problem?

CUSTOMER IN A RESTAURANT: But I ordered Dinosaur Soup!

CUSTOMER IN A RESTAURANT: Waiter!

WAITER: What seems to be the problem, madam?

CUSTOMER IN A RESTAURANT: There doesn't seem to be any pterodactyl in this Pterodactyl Soup.

WAITER: So? There isn't any dog in a dog biscuit, either.

CUSTOMER IN A RESTAURANT: Waiter, there's a brontosaurus in my soup!

WAITER: So what's the problem?

CUSTOMER IN A RESTAURANT: I ordered Allosaurus Soup.

CUSTOMER IN A RESTAURANT: Waiter! There's a
dinosaur in my soup!
WAITER: Don't yell so loudly. Everyone will want one.

CUSTOMER IN A RESTAURANT: Why is there a
tyrannosaurus rex in my soup?
WAITER: The chef ran out of flies.

CUSTOMER IN A RESTAURANT: Waiter!
WAITER: What's the matter, madam?
CUSTOMER IN A RESTAURANT: What is this
brontosaurus doing in my soup?
WAITER: Looks to me like he's doing the backstroke.

CUSTOMER IN A RESTAURANT: Why is there a dead
dinosaur in my soup?
WAITER: The heat kills them.

CUSTOMER IN A RESTAURANT: What's the hardest part
about making dinosaur soup?
WAITER: Stirring it.

CUSTOMER IN A RESTAURANT: Waiter, there's a dinosaur in my soup!

WAITER: Don't worry. The soup's not deep enough to drown him.

CUSTOMER IN A RESTAURANT: Waiter, there's a dinosaur in my soup!

WAITER: Don't worry, madam. We won't charge extra.

CUSTOMER IN A RESTAURANT: Waiter, there's a dinosaur in my soup!

WAITER: Don't worry, madam. The soup's not hot enough to burn him.

CUSTOMER IN A RESTAURANT: Waiter, there's a dinosaur in my soup!

WAITER: It was a last minute substitution. We couldn't find a fly.

CUSTOMER IN A RESTAURANT: Waiter, there's a stegosaurus in my soup!

WAITER: No need to show off your knowledge of paleontology.

CUSTOMER IN A RESTAURANT: Waiter! There's a dead dinosaur in my soup.

WAITER: What do you expect for these prices? A live one?

CUSTOMER IN A RESTAURANT: What's this animal in my soup?

WAITER: I don't know, sir. I can't tell one dinosaur from another.

CUSTOMER IN A RESTAURANT: There's a dead stegosaurus in the butter.

WAITER: I beg to differ.

CUSTOMER IN A RESTAURANT: I tell you, there's a dead stegosaurus in the butter.

WAITER: Wrong again.

CUSTOMER IN A RESTAURANT: What do you mean?

WAITER: For one thing, that's not a dead stegosaurus. It's a dead brontosaurus. For another thing, that's not butter. That's two-week-old mashed potatoes.

CHAPTER FIVE

High, Wide, and Woolly

Woolly Mammoths and
Mastodons Ride Again

CHAIM: Let's pretend.
RACHEL: Pretend what?
CHAIM: Let's pretend you were given a baby woolly mammoth.
RACHEL: Okay. Now what?
CHAIM: How would you raise it?
RACHEL: With a hydraulic lift.

CUSTOMER IN A RESTAURANT: Waiter, there's a hair in my soup.
WAITER: Black or brown? We seem to be missing a woolly mammoth.

RUTH: What was the biggest moth of all time?
PAUL: I give up.
RUTH: The mam-moth.

ANDREW: How do you prevent a woolly mammoth from going through the eye of a needle?
SUE: Tie a knot in its tail.

EVAN SPENCER: What's the difference between a very old shaggy mammoth and a dead bee?
MICHAEL ELIOT: What?
EVAN SPENCER: One's a seedy beast, while the other's a deceased bee.

What happened to the woolly mammoth when she crashed through the screen door?
    She strained herself.

Why did the woolly mammoth paint the bottoms of his feet brown?

So no one could see him when he sat upside down in the jar of peanut butter.

RACHEL: How can you tell if a woolly mammoth is hiding under your bed?

ADAM: How?

RACHEL: Your nose is squashed against the ceiling.

PAUL: Who is the largest player on the New York Yankees?

RUTH: MastoDON Mattingly. He hits a ton.

What do you get when you cross a woolly mammoth with a penguin?

I don't know, but I know one thing, it's in a very tight-fitting tuxedo.

What do you get when you cross a woolly mammoth with a cat?

A town that is free of dogs.

Why don't woolly mammoths go swimming at the beach?

They can't keep their trunks up.

What's the difference between a woolly mammoth and a flea?

A woolly mammoth can have a flea, but a flea can't have a woolly mammoth.

What did the woolly mammoth say when it lost its trunk?

Tusk, tusk.

LESLIE: Can a woolly mammoth jump very high?
LORNA: Are you kidding? He can barely clear his throat.

WOOLLY MAMMOTH #1: Why are you putting that ear of corn on top of the taxi?

WOOLLY MAMMOTH #2: I wanted corn on the cab.

CUSTOMER IN A RESTAURANT: Can I have some mammoth steak on rye, please?

WAITER: With pleasure!

CUSTOMER IN A RESTAURANT: No, with ketchup.

Knock, knock.
Who's there?
Turner.
Turner who?
   Turner round, there's a mastodon breathing down your neck.

MASTODON #1: How old are you?

MASTODON #2: I just turned 56.

MASTODON #1: Ah. 65!

MASTODON #1: Do you know the name of that woolly mammoth over there?

MASTODON #2: Art.

MASTODON #1: Art who?

MASTODON #2: Artesian.

MASTODON #1: Ah! I know Artesian well.

WOOLLY MAMMOTH #1: I'm so sore from running, I can neither stand nor sit.

WOOLLY MAMMOTH #2: If what you say is true, you must be lying.

WOOLLY MAMMOTH #1: How come the Beasts of Baluchistan are so good-natured?

WOOLLY MAMMOTH #2: They have to be.

WOOLLY MAMMOTH #1: Why?

WOOLLY MAMMOTH #2: Because they can't fight and they can't run.

ADAM: Why are there no woolly mammoths in the Caribbean Islands?

RACHEL: Why?

ADAM: They couldn't afford the airfare.

DOROTHY: What do you get when you cross a woolly mammoth with a porcupine?

TONI: A very cross porcupine.

WOOLLY MAMMOTH: The flies are thick around here.

DIMETRODON: You shouldn't talk like that. You're not so smart yourself.

TOBY: How do you get down off a woolly mammoth?

TED: You find yourself a ladder and climb down.

TOBY: Nope.

TED: You strap on a parachute and jump.

TOBY: Nope.

TED: You buy 50 helium balloons and float off.

TOBY: Nope.

TED: I give up. How do you get down off a woolly mammoth?

TOBY: You don't get down off a woolly mammoth. You get *down* off a duck.

What is dark brown on the inside and clear on the outside?
   A woolly mammoth in a baggy.

DON: What do you get when you cross a woolly
   mammoth with a kangaroo?
COREY: What?
DON: I don't know, but whatever it is, whenever it
   jumps up and down, it leaves huge holes in your
   lawn.

Knock, knock.
Who's there?
Ron.
Ron who?
   Ron a little faster, because I see a mastodon
over there.

ADAM: What do you get
   when you cross a woolly
   mammoth with a parrot?
RACHEL: What?
ADAM: I don't know what to call it, but when it asks
   for a cracker, you better give it one.

DEBORAH: Do we get fur from woolly mammoths?
IVY: Yes, we get as fur from them as we can.

CHAPTER SIX

The Stegosauruses Meet the Allosauruses

(Oh Well, You Can't Expect Everybody to Get Along)

What do you call an allosaurus that's not feeling well?
   An illosaurus.

ALLOSAURUS #1: Gee, I hope I'm sick and have to go
   to the doctor.
ALLOSAURUS #2: Now, why would you say a foolish
   thing like that?
ALLOSAURUS #1: Because I would hate to be well
   and feel this rotten.

ALLOSAURUS #1: I'm leaving this swamp and not
   coming back.
ALLOSAURUS #2: Why?
ALLOSAURUS #1: Because of illness.
ALLOSAURUS #2: Because of illness?
ALLOSAURUS #1: Yeah. All the other dinosaurs are
   sick and tired of me.

JEFF: Why does the allosaurus lie on its back with its
   feet pointed toward the sky?
KATE: I give up. Why does the allosaurus lie on its
   back with its feet pointed toward the sky?
JEFF: So it can trip up pterodactyls.

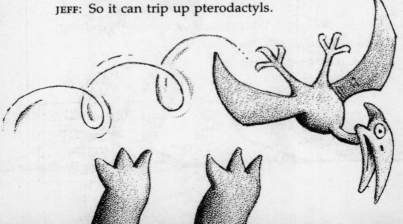

MOTHER ALLOSAURUS: My son has decided to take up acting.

FATHER ALLOSAURUS: What's so bad about that?

MOTHER ALLOSAURUS: Well, he weighs so much that, whenever he appears in a play, he crashes right through the floor.

FATHER ALLOSAURUS: Don't worry about that. It's just a stage he's going through.

FATHER ALLOSAURUS: I think I have chronic indigestion.

MOTHER ALLOSAURUS: You probably just ate somebody who disagreed with you.

FATHER ALLOSAURUS: Do you like eating human brains?

MOTHER ALLOSAURUS: At least it gives one food for thought.

What should you look for if you bring home an allosaurus as a pet?
Your insurance policy.

Let's try that again. What should you look for if you bring home an allosaurus as a pet?
A new place to live.

What wears earrings, has purple hair, and weighs two tons?
   A punk allosaurus.

What does an allosaurus do on Thanksgiving Day?
   Give thanks that it is not a turkey.

ALLOSAURUS, JR.: Hey, Dad, did you know that I do bird impressions?
ALLOSAURUS, SR.: No, I didn't. What do you do?
ALLOSAURUS, JR.: I eat worms.

MOTHER ALLOSAURUS: Junior just ran away with the circus.
FATHER ALLOSAURUS: Tell him to bring it back.

ALLOSAURUS, JR.: I know a dinosaur that lays square eggs that weigh over 100 pounds apiece.
MOTHER ALLOSAURUS: Well, that is something, all right.
ALLOSAURUS, JR.: But that's not all. That dinosaur can talk, as well.
MOTHER ALLOSAURUS: Talk, as well? I find that difficult to believe. What does it say?
ALLOSAURUS, JR.: Ouch! OUCH!

Although the stegosaurus was about 20 feet long and weighed up to 4 tons, its brain was probably no bigger than a walnut. Thus, he spawned quite a few jokes:

Why did the stegosaurus take a four-leaf clover from his 600-page book?
   He had been pressing his luck too long.

Why did the stegosaurus run around and around his bed?
   He was trying to catch up with his sleep.

Why did the stegosaurus go to night school?
   He wanted to be able to read in the dark.

STEGOSAURUS: What's that awful thing on your neck?
ALLOSAURUS: I don't know. Get it off me!
STEGOSAURUS: I can't. It's your head.

STEGOSAURUS: Man, you're a stupid-looking creature.
ALLOSAURUS: Hey! I didn't come here to be insulted.
STEGOSAURUS: Okay. Where do you usually go to be insulted?

TEACHER: Now, if you had two stegosaurus fossils in the La Brea tar pits, and you found two allosaurus fossils in the same tar pit, how many fossils would you have?

NANCY: Now that's what I call a sticky problem.

Why did the stegosaurus wear spikes all the time?
    Because he wanted to be a sharp dresser.

Who is the stegosaurus's favorite baseball player?
    Spike Owens.

Who was the stegosaurus's favorite musical performer?
    Spike Jones.

LAUREN: What do you get if you cross a stegosaurus with a cow?

NANCY: I give up. What?

LAUREN: Milk that's too terrifying to drink.

Why don't the dinosaurs allow the stegosaurus to play baseball with them?

Because he's always spiking the other players.

Why didn't the stegosaurus ask the brontosaurus to the dance at the La Brea tar pits?

He was going to, but at the last moment he got coal feet.

DO YOU DO THE BRONTO' BOUNCE?

STEGOSAURUS #1: You really shouldn't eat that window.

STEGOSAURUS #2: Why not?

STEGOSAURUS #1: You'll end up with a pane in your stomach.

STEGOSAURUS #1: Talk to me of winter.
STEGOSAURUS #2: Why? It'll go in one year and out the other.

STEGOSAURUS #1: Don't eat the writer of joke books.
STEGOSAURUS #2: Why not?
STEGOSAURUS #1: You'll end up with author-itis.

What did the stegosaurus do when he ripped his pants?
He took them to the dino-sewer.

ELIZA: I just saw a very magical dinosaur.
WILL: What do you mean by a magical dinosaur?
ELIZA: Well, one moment he was a stegosaurus. The next moment he turned into the meadow.

CHAPTER SEVEN

Let's Wing It!

Pterodactyls and
Pteranodons on Parade

IAN: How did you feel when you saw your very first pteranodon flying overhead?

MATTHEW: Ptterrified.

PTERODACTYL #1: I ate too many cantaloupes this morning.

PTERODACTYL #2: How do you feel?

PTERODACTYL #1: Melon-choly.

PTERANODON #1: How come you're completely bald?

PTERANODON #2: From worry.

PTERANODON #1: What do you worry about?

PTERANODON #2: Losing all my hair.

ICTHYOSAURUS: What were you doing with those pterodactyls this morning?

ICTHYOSAURUS , JR.: Oh, they taught me a game that was invented by a tribe in Africa.

ICTHYOSAURUS: Zulus?

ICTHYOSAURUS, JR.: No. Actually, I won.

MARK: What do you call a flying reptile that has a wingspan of 25 feet, toothless jaws, and goes round and round and round?

OONA: A 33 and a ⅓ r.p.m. pteranodon on a record player.

Knock, knock.
Who's there?
Dozen.
Dozen who?

Dozen anybody here know how to spell pterodactyl?

EMILY: How do you know there's a pterodactyl in your refrigerator?
PETE: I don't know. How?
EMILY: You can't close the door.

AULETTA: If you had three pterodactyls in the kitchen, which one would be like a cowboy?
MILGROM: The one on the range.

Knock, knock.
Who's there?
Consumption.
Consumption who?

Consumption be done about all of these pterodactyl jokes?

What do you get when you cross a pterodactyl with a parrot?

A flying dinosaur capable of giving interviews.

FATHER OF A PTERODACTYL: You look pretty dirty, son.

PTERODACTYL, JR.: If you think I look pretty when I'm dirty, you should see how much prettier I look when I'm clean.

DICK: What's the difference between a doughnut and a pterodactyl?

SARAH: Yeah, that's what I say—what's the difference?

DICK: No, no. Come on. Be a sport. What's the difference between a pterodactyl and a doughnut?

SARAH: I give up.

DICK: You can't dip a pterodactyl in your coffee.

SARAH: If I were big enough and if the coffee cup were big enough, I could!

EVELYN: What do you get if you cross the number zero with a pterodactyl?

EILEEN: What?

EVELYN: Nothing—but at least it has wings.

DON: What do pterodactyls have that no other prehistoric animals have?

VIRGINIA: What?

DON: Baby pterodactyls.

PTERODACTYL, JR.: Quick, I need 1,000 gallons of milk.

MOTHER: What for?

PTERODACTYL, JR.: My father wants me to take a bath.

MOTHER: Good idea. You want it pasteurized?

PTERODACTYL, JR.: No. Up to my chin will be fine.

LOU: What is a pterodactyl's favorite drink?

LILLIAN: I give up. What?

LOU: Saur milk.

LILLIAN: Then tell me who would be the pterodactyl's favorite New York Yankees baseball player of all time?

LOU: I give up. Who?

LILLIAN: Hank Saur.

KATHY: What do you get if you cross a pterodactyl with a parrot?

ROBERT: What?

KATHY: A creature that bites off your head when you offer it a cracker.

PTERODACTYL #1: Let's fly down and play with some tops.

PTERODACTYL #2: Tops? What tops?

PTERODACTYL #1: Triceratops, of course.

PTERODACTYL #1: Boy, it's great to live in times like these.

PTERODACTYL #2: Why?

PTERODACTYL #1: Because we don't have to study any history!

PTERODACTYL #1: What dinosaur knows more synonyms than any other?

PTERODACTYL #2: Thesaurus.

PTERODACTYL #1: What's that?

PTERODACTYL #2: A turtle.

PTERODACTYL #1: Oh? For a moment, I thought it was a lizard driving a mobile home.

PTERODACTYL #1: I'm going to take up biology and cross an icthyosaurus with an iguanodon.

PTERODACTYL #2: So what? I'm going to take up fishing and cross a brook and a stream.

What do you get if you cross a pteranodon with a snowman?
Frostbite.

How do you get a pteranodon into a box of matches?
Take the matches out first.

PTERANODON MOTHER: Why did you push your father into the glacier?

PTERANODON, JR.: I was thirsty.

PTERANODON MOTHER: You were thirsty?

PTERANODON, JR.: Yes. I wanted a frozen pop.

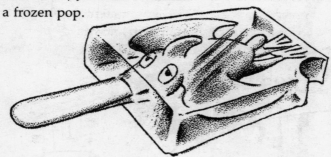

PTERANODON, JR.: Let's fly over the garbage dump.

PTERANODON MOTHER: Don't talk rubbish.

PTERODACTYL: Want to see me imitate a bumblebee?

PTERANODON: Buzz off.

Knock, knock.
Who's there?
Dismay.
Dismay who?
   Dismay be the very last dinosaur
joke in the whole book.